Spirit Journey

Philip Wesley Comfort

2nd Enlarged Edition

Wipf & Stock
PUBLISHERS
Eugene, Oregon

Wipf and Stock Publishers
199 West 8th Avenue, Suite 3
Eugene, Oregon 97401

Spirit Journey
By Comfort, Philip W
Copyright©2003 by Comfort, Philip Wesley
ISBN 13: 978-1-59244-654-4
ISBN 10: 1-59244-654-X
Publication date 9/1/2007
Previously published by Feather Books, UK, 2003

INTRODUCTION

The poems in this volume span a forty-year period—from the year 1967 to 2007. The poems are dated and often have a short explanatory note. Though the poems could be appreciated without these notations, I like to think they are helpful signposts of my spiritual journey.

In the 1960s I wrote many poems, very few of which are included here. There are two good reasons. First, most of that poetry strongly reflected the influence of other poets I was attempting to imitate (particularily Dylan Thomas), while trying to discover my own voice and style. Second, I burned all my poetry after becoming a Christian in May of 1970. This included some of the poems I wrote in 1969–1970, for which I received an award during my freshman year at Kent State University (1969–1970). Part of the honor was to spend a few days with Gary Snyder, the beat poet turned zen.

After I became a Christian, I did not write any poetry for five years. I finally broke my poetic silence in 1975, when I wrote a few spiritual meditations. In the 1980s I was motivated to write some verse because I (and several Christian friends) had been extremely involved with a Christian movement that eventually went bad and hurt many people. This experience evoked many poems, some of which are published here. Among them, the poem "Young men see visions; old men dream dreams" evinced tears among many of my friends.

In 1989, my wife Georgia was diagnosed with breast cancer; in

1

1990 the cancer spread to her bones. During this period and shortly thereafter, as she recovered from radical treatment, I was constantly writing poems. In the following years, she and I befriended many women who struggled with cancer and died. As a consequence, I wrote many poems "in memorium" during the 1990s and early 2000s.

In the same period, I have re–focused my poetic energies on the wonders of nature, spiritual experience, and personal tributes. I have also recreated a few poems I wrote in the late 1960s and in 1970, as best as I could remember them. I felt I needed to do this to give a fuller poetic picture of my spiritual journey – from one who started out as a panthiest and pacifist, experiencing such events as Woodstock and Kent State, and then became a Christian. For the past thirty years I have been on a journey to understand myself, our Creator, my fellow creatures, and Christ. These poems are reflections of that journey.

The Second Edition

The second edition of *Spirit Journey* has 36 new poems (71-106), written from 2003-2007. Some of these were previously included in two poetry collections: "they sang our souls to heaven," "zoa," "excarnate," and "when I came here as spirit" in Feather Books' *Poetry Church Collections*; "he moves" in *Words of Faith*. Three poems in the first edition were later printed in *Pilgrimages* (ed. W. Nash): "until kingdomCome," "IXΘYC" and "Lazarus speaks." Several poems in the second edition are "encomia" for those who have passed on: "fresh fields fill your hands" (for my good friend and neighbor Jim Ellermeier); "your questions now answered" (for my dear uncle John Comfort); "they sang our souls to heaven" (for Bill Haubrich); "for J. D." (my friend and co-editor J. D. Douglas); "passage" (for my friend and fellow member of the team that trans-lated the *New Living Translation*, Kenneth Taylor); and "graced" (for Bruce Metzger, good friend and New Testament scholar).

2

CONTENTS page

1. glory going

as her golden ghost was sinking
into earth's body with exhausted breath
those who knew had come to look death

in this last glimpse of nourished warmth
two boys flickered. quickly. then flew from the earth
their bodies melting into soft candle slivers

while I stand strange, candling colors, and shiver.
dusk glows with a fiercer light than dawn:
it is the fantastic leaving of souls, it is the glory going,

then gone, as when cathedral candles are snuffed
and smell strange in a dark room. I am left alone
and for the first time know he was here and gone

summer 1967

(in memorium for the Hitchcok boys,
especially Ray, my roomate at Choate, 1966–1967,
whose death awakened me to God)

2. Woodstock

from Ohio to New York I hitchhiked
diggin' the journey as much as the end
all on the way the people were chill
and so was the rolling grass and farms
in the middle of nowhere unharmed
as my longhaired kind flocked there
from every wind, a migration to eden,
a heaven of free music and love. man,
the sounds grooved and moved us—
Santana's syncopation, Hendrick's purple haze,
the Who's drivin' rhythm, singing our generation,
chantin' with Country Joe, "Hell, no! we won't go!"
wailin' with Janice Joplin, rockin' with Joe Cocker
swayin' with the mood of Credence Clearwater
movin' with Zepplin up the stairway to heaven
and gettin' so much higher with Sly and the Family Stone!
all night our music rocked long and we rolled with it
as if there were no tomorrow and nowhere else to go –
and when the rains didn't stop, they didn't drop our mood
for we celebrated brotherhood (God is love)
in woods wet with mud and groove

August 1969

Woodstock, New York

8

3.   search for cover

I search for cover
from piercing eyes
a coved cave to hide
sloshed with waves.
if a prophet wants
to speak to me
let him chant the wind.
Zarathustra, stay away
Siddartha Guatama, don't say
you've found thirstless bliss
for Jesus came as water

December 1969

4. Kent State

sun turned black moon bloodred
over seven wounded and four dead –
can't you see them lying past those bayonettes
under the haze of smoking guns and teargas stain?
can't you see her hands outstretched
as she wails to the wind. to anyone. to God.
to defend. to explain. to take revenge!
no prayer can bring them back
these innocent rebels cut down at Kent,
unintended unadorned martyrs
by a reign that refuses to mourn, refuses regret
for a generation that must – by God – be cracked

May 4, 1970

(in memorium of the Kent State shootings
my freshman year at Kent)

5. I was a generation

I was a generation unfurled, a mad prophet unscrolled
ripping our straight world with an outpouring of questions
I cut free from Christianity America and war
(no more would I die because they said so)
finding God in woods, lyrics, and hallucinogenics
I had a band of hippies preaching love on every campus
I gloried at woodstock, ommed with zen, tuned out and in again
till I was jarred by Nam, ripped off in Haight, and wounded at Kent
I couldn't sing my way back to the garden again
because I died one night in a Frisco gym –
while the Dead plucked on and stoned heads toked smoke
to Oregon, greened by mountain streams, I treked
having heard Jesus was hiding in the same tall winds
that said he was hanging out somewhere still and cool

late May, 1970

(two weeks after the Kent State shooting, just after I hitchhiked to
San Francisco and arrived at a Christian commune in Quines
Creek, Oregon)

11

6. siphon the sweet

vintaged
he was crushed
he was must
he was juice
fermenting

I, wine thief,
a rebel
siphoned
the sweet

when I
didn't even
deserve
the lees

summer 1975

7. so many Jesuses

with its Bibles abandoned in the back corner
and iconographic gadgets hanging over the front counter
that overlooks the rows of idle aisles
hungover with the aroma of incense catholitizing the air
that's filled with hallowed light and holy tunes –
makes me feel wholly unholy
though I know I shouldn't feel that way
with so many Jesuses staring at me
with big blue American eyes
but I can't help it
it makes me sick as sunday school
and my Christ inside nearly dies
every time I enter you
oh yes, I know it's all so nice
Tyndale wouldn't have to die for this
and Wycliffe could come back from exile
to be put on the biographical shelf
next to all the commentaries on Jeremiah
who still weeps for you

December 1977

8. dried flowers

when the light in the word
has become too familiar
and the Songs are dried flowers
in a romantic memoir
and I have read about kisses
but not kissed any lips,
then I stop my labor
and come to him, the ark of my heart
to be carried through the river.
I will go under and come up
a new lover of God
having the sweetness
of the smell of sacrifice
as in the burning of old poems and books—
oh to be lit by Jesus Christ
and melted by his looks!

January 1978

9. young men see visions. old men dream dreams

1

young men dreamed dreams and saw visions
even felt heard tasted for a moment
eternity descend into humanity
a foretaste of new Jerusalem
where unity among brothers was reality
not legislated or mandated
but spirated by holy miraculous breath

all breathed the same pneuma
charged divine with purpose and plan
all joined to sing the same tune
and stepped to the same beat
an army marching into victory.
we thought we were about to recover
the pristine glory of the early ecclesia
lost for generations now revealed to ours

but when the dark came out
we lost sight of Christ and mistook the light
the vision blurred, the dream shattered
and the joy of unity was turned
into the dread of monolithic conformity
those who heard different voices
were like the old prophets stoned
and those who kept the memory of that distant tune
went insane trying to remember the words

2

we tried to achieve what we couldn't
and struggled not to become history
we yearned for freedom from ancestry
for liberation from the cycle
of insidious recapitulation
but man makes man more like himself
with each passing generation
whoever has tried to break the trend
has had to bend to bend to bend
until broken into useless fragments

oh Jesus, could you love this debris?
would you repair these broken minds
and make them vessels full of glory
or write upon these shattered ostraca
a lasting living redacted story?
could you build upon the ruins
from the rubble of shattered stones
a temple for visitation
to which, O Lord, you'd come?

don't leave us each alone, Jesus God,
as scattered desert bones
never formed again into an army
each, with our own treacherous war
fighting tears and years of isolation
struggling for sanity and sanctity
as we await reconstitution—
and yet if you are with us, it is enough,
for you promised nothing else

summer 1983

after the fall of the recovery

10.   no other way

to me there is no other way
if I would follow him

a broken heart brought me to Jesus
a cracked soul keeps me bent

I have felt the wounds
from those I called my friends

I have been forsaken
by those I came to trust

when I've cried for justice
he opened not his mouth

when I asked for reasons
he pointed to the cross

I hate there was a murder
and no funeral for the loss

December 6, 1985

11. bring eden back

we thought we'd bring eden back
like dawn and dove and ghost
we hoped we could make it last
and flourish like a rose
but flowers drop in autumn
and birds wing after the sun
the gray melts into waters
whose dying waves never end.
perhaps a dolphin will ride the surf
and on his back a dead man come
who's risen from the abyss –
he'll mystify our deepest thoughts
when he prophecies there is no death
and life is second birth

June 22, 1988

12. you are loved

you are loved not because
your form's immortal
(an ancient marbled goddess)
nor because you've mansioned heaven
where time is still and tears dry.
wounded, your spirit inspires muses
and lifts God's souls to highest art
and air that others sing –
a musician's dream in living being.
you have moved me with the beauty
of one who found her soul in him
who once piped mystic strains
to the blind and deaf and dumb

February 22, 1989

(to Georgia on the day of her masechtomy
for breast cancer)

19

13. deliverance

in the sedateness of our spirits
where anger doesn't roar
we've heard a throbbing voice
that speaks "live more, live more"

while the aging, aching body cries
and screams for its deliverance
the Spirit sent from heaven's Son
gives grace for perseverance

cursed creation bent with labor
doubled in writhing pain
has pushed its head, the savior, out
but the body still remains

September 1989

14. let not

O Jesus God her Savior

let not my lover yield to death
flash. quicken. infuse breath.
appear! reveal! suddenly come
with fresh infused regeneration
creating life from cell to cell
make faith! (faith makes all things well)

presence yourself within her body
make it clean and sweep it holy
fuse the wounds that touched your soul
and caused you, Lord, to go through hell
for you have risen from those pains
but can't forget that we remain

O Jesus our Savior God

October 16, 1989

(when my wife was diagnosed
with further metastasis of cancer)

21

15. move alone

a monarch makes solo flight
driven by instinct and light
    a salmon strokes upstream
    dying to spill its sperm
        a turtle hatched on shore
        seeks the sea for its mother

        once the union has been broken
        life is hell split from heaven
I can't tell where I'm going
I only know that I am gone
I can't stop till I've found you
for I too long have moved alone

late October 1989

22

16. a Gideon's Bible

you lie in bed
I sit by you
squeezing your hand
as I look
at a Gideon's Bible
on your bedstand
and a sainted nurse
gracefully handling
an awful machine
pumping poison
into your veins.
we all sense
his presence
over all
and feel
no contradiction.

March 16, 1990

(to my wife, Georgia, on her first day
of chemotherapy)

17.   the Arbiter

as I watched her life
hang in the balance
and slump under hung weight
I begged the Arbiter
to lift oppression
and restore her wasted health.
down I bowed to the ground
and asked him who died for her
to rise for her
to call the marrow
and tomorrow into being

if he didn't hear the spirit
of a thousand warring prayers
he must have felt the plaintive moan
of motherless sons, the pointed plea
piercing sense and sensibility,
for he multiplied his hosts
to form a grafted force
against the insidious enemy –
germ fought germ in fervent war
until her fever lifted

what moved his hand
to tip the scale
is not clear to me or visible
was it praying saints
or dreadful fevers?
was it a child's anguish
of losing his mother?
all I know is she was touched
and given glory's extra weight.
she sprang to life and I rose up
to praise the God of mercy

April 5, 1990   (ten days after my wife's
bonemarrow transplant)

24

18. Lazarus speaks

      after Lazarus was raised
he said nothing we know of
he didn't write a book
or go on tour
he just sat there
      he didn't speak
of paradise or hades
and didn't say
if he was glad
to be back
      Mary and Martha thrilled
and so did Jersualem
but the leaders
wanted him stilled as a tomb
in case he had a story

July 1990

25

19. think of nothing

I sit beneath
an apple tree
in August
breathing heat
feeling sun
sinking into green

beetles unaware
of my presence
couple and mate
while a yellowjacket
pollinates pansies

cicadas stroke the air
carrying a dog's bark
that marks the distance
from there to here
where I sit
and think of nothing

August 9, 1990

26

20.   a man's mind

nature is regular
except for the wind.
apple trees
are white in May
green in June
red in September
black in December.
a man's mind
after many changes
is still

summer 1990

21. this sad madness

everyone I've read
is dead
the raving poets
mad at time
the tired theologians
worn for words
the crazed mystics
charged with lies
   they all swore at the curse
and called for an end
to this sad madness
   but no one shouting epithets
has demythologized the epitaphs
and no one anathematizing death
has been left to pronounce its doom
it still comes
swiftly to some
an arrow shot in the heart
while to others it drags on
a mouse tossed in a cat's paws
before the kill
   yet there are others
who've seen it coming all along
and like a cornered mongoose
strike the moccasin
before it forks its tongue

November 7, 1990
(the day Brenda Stahr was buried)

28

22. thoughts they didn't say

entire civilizations wiped out
like chalkboard notes
with no trace left
of lovers kissing in the dark –
only cold stone obelisks
boasting of wars and prisoners
some ancient lyrics
survived their lover's lips
in papyrus scraps and codices
and one can almost hear
Odysseus whisper love
to Penelope
but tongues that sparked fire
through the night
lie silent in the grave
and all that's left
is words about love
and thoughts they didn't say

November 1990

23. there are times

there are times
when all is well
when even winter seems right
and darkness is peaceful like music

and there are times
when my spirit feels slightly stirred
by his presence—
I didn't ask for him to come
only for repose from madness
this too is good and unexpected

and there are times
when rest is good
sleep, a blessing
writing, a happy chore
when I am content
with my wife, work, and children

and there are times
precious times
that seem fewer as my days slink longer
when I sense eternity
is near me
looking over my shoulder
with a smile

sometimes – most times – I let it pass
but once in a while
I understand and laugh

December 1990

24. panegyric for Georgia, Colette, Barb

the Greeks like moderns
celebrated the games
and sang of them in panegyric poems.
the winners were heroes
eulogized in Olympic odes
immortalized above the gods.
the marathoner was the best of them
if he could outlast the rest
the wreath he earned would never fade
because its garland was laud and praise.
but what of those unsung
who were forced to run a marathon
or claw for survival in wild arenas
and battle invisible odds?
what crown is given them
for wrestling reason and slaying giants,
for testing limits and trying time?
if they fall we drop a petal on their grave
and grieve their falling as our own
but if they rise they flower praise
and wear the victor's sprouting ring
a laureate of grace and peace
for those triumphant, tired, and meek.

March 18, 1991

31

25. I've missed them

friends return to my mind
lost ones
like the first break of spring
with hint of warm wind.
Jesus, I've missed them
and the times we laughed at nothing.
the blankness in between has been
a long Chicago winter
where the sun is hardly seen
and memories, matter.

March 1, 1992

(for Dan, Eric, Rick, Verne)

26. speak peace

elk bound softpawed through white aspen
black bear paw rainbow trout from streams

all ears to the symphonic river
that smooths rocks and signals sun
all eyes to the hungry hunted
who escape the fleet, swoop, and tongue

an unburrowed groundhog spies enemies
a magpie glides on upward draft

all ears to the snaredrum thunder
that scares mares and spooks rain
all eyes to the hoarhead peaks
that speak peace to those insane

June 1992

(Beaver Creek, Colorado)

33

27. plowed under

he didn't care what they were before
the rows of furrowed souls plowed under
whether plump grains of full stature
or slim seeds shriveled to the core
all lay silent with no moment of their own
those buried in cinders and those in stone.
over the sleeping seeded plain
storms have come and suns have gone
yet not one has split the depressed sod.
some think flowers bloom in heaven's garden
picked stealthily from sunken graves by God
others scoff at eternal paradise
and call on hope to give it up.
but prophets shout harvest will come
when heads break sudden glory
abandoning their rotten rinds
as monarchs shedding split cocoons!

March 1994

28. tribute to my father

my father,
though you've never pushed me on some appointed way
your meekness, for which the new earth waits,
attracts me to follow like night comes after day.
I am solaced in your simple presence
as you suffuse my worries without fierce words.
your spirit, unnaturally joyous, gladdens my face—
and when I haven't even thought of God, you inspire praise

July 22, 1994

(in celebration of my father's seventieth birthday)

29. it doesn't make any kind sense

hope hangs on her last gasps
that mother will again laugh
that wife can somehow outpain the last
but damn silence obituates,
while angels once again watch
Apollyon work as sovereign.
why must some go, some stay
parted by incomprehensibleness?
it doesn't make any kind sense
that a hallowed glow has sped to spirit
while hollowness haunts lives poked slow

December 2, 1994

(in memorium for Colette)

30. epiphany

I'm told seraphim once hallowed earth
in shapes that stretched surreal
they took meals with common folk
and rescued them from certain hell.
I haven't seen celestials wing through trees
but I eyed your blonde soul moving near
and recognized an angel in the flesh
with otherwomanness moving sacred spheres.
I haven't touched a spirit so daring to give
to daunt sure death and devotedly live –
this, my love, is witness to the truth
that heaven hasn't stopped gracing earth.

Christmas 1994

(for Georgia, my wife)

31. roadkill requiem

for the flattened fox
whose tail still wags in the highway wind
for the smeared skunk gut–spilled
the squashed cat and splattered squirrel
    say something for them in solemn tones
for the gushed crow–pecked groundhog
the mangled rabbit in dry blood
the decapitated snake and wasted wren
    the unconvicted must pray something anguished
for the eviscerated deer with stunned eyes
the stifflegged dog and dumb possum—
    say something for the unburied unburrowed masses
who've died while making natural crosses
    let's pray Ezekiel to slip from the dead
and breathe into their gaping jaws
that they may earth our forests again,
O God!

July 20, 1995

38

32. who can be certain?

    can we stalk the invisible and murder it in the row
can we shuck the hardened peel and peer inside the veil
where he trespassed edges/sceptered space
wedged firmaments/moved zones into untamed spheres?
    if we could pin the infinite end
we'd compass the way in swift stroke
but nothing we know is perfect/straight/round
unlike sense/sound/light it does not curve or bend
    even the runnings on my palms fall off the edge
who can be certain that what's now leads to then?
anticipation of lips may be sweeter than the kiss
and thirst tastier than savored wine

November 29, 1995

33. Grace

a long lingering kiss, a polite goodbye
she got herself ready to meet him
while we wouldn't release our grasp
when the call came to leave the waiting
she was glad he had not forgot
(though it's hard to part from memory)
she gently pushed away from us
and eloped to another's love
as spoke the smile on her parted lips
a heavened wife, her marriage is now the best
for Grace has come to consummation
in a scene she always desired to brush

January 21, 1996

(in memorium: the day after my grandmother's death,
Dorothy Grace Bigham)

34. swerve

light can't be stopped
                         it bends around trees
           like a corner kick
nor is water dammed
                            swerving around walls
                 like a mad striker
                            it violates the goal

always curves and flows

no straight line rivers my maps
                          the crooked is divine
   zigs and zags   are expected
even the long penciled stroke on the sea's horizon
is a myth

but humans
   like perfection
keep straining
to
go
straight
up
the
middle

June 1, 1996

35. Lookout Mountain

another sacred moment
just blew in with the western wind
the trees moved like water
the leaves sounded like river
as we ascended Lookout Mountain
into thinner air and thicker blue
we spoke of God breaking through the heavens
and speaking with us as with Abraham
but that was then, we concluded
as we moved around another bend
pausing now and again to enjoy the interplay
of shade and light on undulating glade

we climbed on, taking switchbacks here and there
unhurried we stopped to let some hikers pass –
you asked if the word was true
that all our sins are gone if we confess
to which I said "they're all forgotten and removed
as far as the east is from the west"
then taking the lead again you swung around an aspen
and I above the rush of clapping leaves
barely heard you say "then we're new"

up we went traversing rocks and fallen elms
circumventing a gnarly pine with exposed roots
to which I said here's a tree that survived
and says to the world I'm here
to which you replied "so am I"
as you took another step up

when we reached the height
we sought our own stone sanctuary
open only to the four winds and seven spirits
where under September sky and sun
God said something sweet and small

we laughed aloud and even howled
as we ran down that mountain trail!

September 21, 1996

(Montreat, North Carolina)

36. disappear

God disappears after the shouted hallelujahs
behind some angel oak tangled in the light
the wind taking him away like brilliant thoughts

I watch clouds fluff, flag as they're eaten by sky
and wonder what I'd do if he rained on me
since I've come to believe in the invisible

the stallion waves come rushing to shore
then disappear just as quickly in the surf
earth is a good place for forever I believe

April 27, 1997

44

37. grasped grace

I'm amazed at the way you take it
as if it were a cup of sweet southern tea
served with lemon slice in ice
sipped slowly under sprawling angel oaks
    you've spoken about it so often
I'm almost used to it –
how you laugh at aging and revere
each metaphorphosis precious
    the confederate jasmine clinging to our trellis
has yet to sprout a mellow bloom
but neither of us are ready to cut it down
for we know of second chances
    stumped trees line our land sprouting fresh branches
jungle magnolia, sweet gums, greening poplars
those tall pines have watched the foxes come and go
while I've marveled at the way your hands open and close
    you'll grasp the grace when it's handed you
for you've touched it already and already know –
while I can only guess the scents of paradise
you've taken back a petal or two

autumn 1997

(for Georgia)

45

38. leaf–turning

forests flattened into books
spirits pressed to verse
have been known to resurrect
in the opening of the pages –
it is then that we taste Taylor's mead
and savor Traherne's pristine spirits;
turning another leaf we slip into the garden
where Milton makes paradise fall and rise
and Hopkins bursts falcons flash flame;
at another turn we find ourselves in the church
where Herbert anneals our stains
and Donne preaches death undone and stung;
at yet another bend we come near the end
where Dickinson knows the transport by the pain
and Dylan rages 'gainst the dying of the light.
these we take with us into the night
their muses tucked between the covers
opened then closed, closed then opened
they grab us now and again and take us
where their papers grow – long thin sheets of it
stories high, already poemed and primed

November 12, 1997

39. no rest

unmarked calendar – no parousia
no anxious buildup to despair
a dog's life on the porch, a frog in my shoe
exploding sun, halfmoon, slim poplar

these have achieved nothing

sailing ships leave no trace of passing through waters
seagulls make no tears in the air they split
the wave I caught and rode smoothly and quickly
heaves no trophy of accomplishment
the wind doesn't wear the smoke it lifts

several people will convince you to make a mark

the southern sunset splatters the sky cool red
in the morning it returns faithful and washed
raining itself over wildwood and meadow
covering everything with wet wash and clean

this is what it means to be effective

when the world was zipped up in chaotic night
luminaries were never known or missed
when earth broke this water it birthed into light
it sprouted greens and humans stretching skyward
with longings longer than sighs

there has never been a perfect place of rest

December 22, 1997

40. drug divine

dripping through pipes immaculate
as turkish opium thick and black
it falls down as night and stains our air
with coats and coats of smoky mere
settling late into the evening mind
suffusing, sedating, stronger than wine,
than sex, and longer than friends
conquering enemies and all that depends.
its sacredness I worship holy
and let it willfully take my body –
as it slurs my thoughts, steals what's tragic
I take its thick mystique and magic.
it opiates anyone at any hour
king culprit crucified or crucifier
it shouldn't be feared and can't be figured
it must be revered as the sweet precursor.
Romans, robbed of it, died wide–eyed
Americans, fighting it, exist deprived
no one can outlaw this soporofic
it's drug divine, sanctioned paregoric

January 9, 1998

48

41. father to son

with all its inconsistencies, worries, and woes
      choose life before it passes into ghost
when affliction tempts you to cease desire
      choose pain over numbness, not ice but fire
do not go until your soul is forged a saint—
      for God, not devil, has the power to create

you're made like me, a man who doubts his best,
      is pained and perplexed by what there's left
to turn on earth before it turns against itself
      I divine you'll find the physician in your soul
then pick leaves that make the nations see
      fulfillment of apocalyptic prophecies

love your Lord, yourself, your brothers,
      cherish your life, your father and mother,
sieze the truth and live it with zeal
      the light is your path, not what you feel
don't grope as I groped for a ladder in the skies
      your road to glory is Jesus Christ

42. ΙΧΘΥC

ΙΧΘΥC was once a sign
on catacombs and martyr's homes
signaling allegiance to the Nazarene.
those who knew him claimed him Christ
and swore – not to Caesar – he was God's Son
the only begotten risen Savior.
Christianoi they called them, humanity's haters
athiests, Oedipists, and Thysteans
secretive, aloof, born of Nazareth's joke
snuffed by Rome for superstition
from Nero to Diocletian they burnt them –
their bodies their bones their books.
Domitian, Trajan, Hadrian purged them
but they refused their noxious incense,
already burning for
IHCOYC
XPICTOC
ΘEOY
YIOC
COTHP
for they'd rather flame than flicker

June 29, 1998

50

43.   beyond our grasp

we are spirit, elohim, inferior only
to cherubim. with elongated wingspans we stretch edges and think we
can fly an unwalled sky in all directions we imagine
but you, God, are DepthBreadthLengthHeight
your reach is incredible SOMUCHSO that we cannot fill our spirits
with you just as we can't swallow any star we see –
oh, you put us at such a grave distance when you breathed us
into flesh (o u r m i n d s f l a s h w a y b e y o n d o u r g r a s p)
we hate that earth encloses our bones but we refuse
to entomb, we rescind to ash. We call on you great God to act:
imp our crimped wings with divine feathers!
rip off the pinions, slit the tethers!

July 1998

51

44. divinity dropped

at nine whether there is sun or none
numbered hymns are sung in coats and ties
the sermon comes predictably interesting
collect, confession, prayers, communion

outside is fresh and blood for me

the sea breaks open bread
            light in me opens
the sky pours wine
            God falls to my tongue
I taste divinity dropped and start to hum

August 1998

52

45. waiting

movement i

black, charcoal black
was the wait of our night
the usual kind of waiting
waiting for something
to be done and over
so that we could know for sure
what we'd been waiting for
it was black still, still black
ebony black, an African mask
bark black, crow black, dead black
blackbird black, forest black
Bible black, priest's garb black
hours passed unmarked hours
no shadow moving up the steps
to count the slow hours
blacker than a cat could see
blacker than satan could make us believe
deep hole black, deepest hole black
with no sign of the next shovelful
turning over anything but black
everything was obsidian
blackness heavier than water
where we remembered our sadness
never the bright
under and above nothing could be heard
but our own limited breathing
there was no hum to music
the tune and message were gone
like winds and memories
but we got used to it
and thought it wasn't as black as before

it was poor black, wornout black
old tar and tiretread black
sloe black very slow black
the black you stumble in
but somehow find the door
it was that kind of black
the blackboard erased again and again
the pencil led dulled to a nub
and just when our eyes got used to it
it turned gray a bit
like the tip of lit charcoal
the ash of a cigarette
the gray of vapid dense fog
wet gray, great ghosts of it
shifting lifting landing drifting
opening closing making us think
we could see through the hovering
but it was nothing more than gray
livid unlit obscure
it was cold gray
broken battleship gray
icelandic autumn gray
it was dirty, defaced
aged tombstones
civil war monuments
worn roads tarred long ago
and tired confederate coats
we didn't know if this gray
was better than the black
it just lasted longer
while we waited for something
to be done and over
so that we could know for sure
what we'd been waiting for
it was like the graying of charcoal

before the orange glow
when a flash–fleck first shows through
then slowly burns away the gray
soaking up in itself
the black, the dark, the haze

movement ii

but it didn't happen as we supposed
just our dun imaginations
wanting something to happen
so we made up blue music
and slurred many gray words
and this made us think we knew
that something would certainly happen
if we could make it color the night
these tunes carried us many a day
while we waited for something
to be done and over
but the songs never slit the haze
even when each of us took off
an unchained star
in private perigrinations
some obscure some dim some unlit
not part of any constellation –
the journey of thought was too quick to collect
too heavy to weigh, too black to paint –
under the sun it was once different
we saw acres of cows roll into hills
scroll into oats, sway like horses' backs
dip and dive pelican–style to ocean's end
these were dimensions we could manuever
we could even find our way around faces
and read them like maps

but everything in darkness changes shape
we desperately painted a pleasant exodus
where we would embrace our lovers at desperate end
and whisper that it was meant to be
but when night took over again
we clutched and screamed,
"no, not this way, not this way to go
into memory into history into obscurity"
tucked away into a pile of papers
fading – because we're supposed to
because we're wrinkled
burdensome and old

movement iii

lasting out the darkness we determined
to grip our beliefs like bibles
while we waited for a slim streak of light
to turn our black to gray and gray to white
but we got old and tainted and swarthy
as dalipidated as collapsing porches
we figured we matched a worn photograph –
unshingled roofs, unpainted boards, broken steps
with sleeping dogs curled around our slanted bones
nothing was going to change and we knew it
the blackness had done this, the murkiness
at one time, we remembered, the pond was lucid
the bottom was clear enough to see the trout
swim between the fallen logs and broken rock
but now the sky was mud
and the earth no better off
our thoughts wandered farther than Moses
offtrack out of step into vultured places
as tough as heaven's door in drought

we stumbled into caves on cliffs
and found ourselves with those named
the sons of light – meaning they were right
to take the dry hills abandoned by jackals
and survive a wasted sea
a perfect place for worn knees, long beards
and waterless prayers swarming the air like flies
they were sure the Teacher would come to them
to scorch their world of religious wrong –
their scribes scripted this strong deliverer
in sacred lines as tight as goatskin
while on the other side of parchment cliffs
where light comes down like paper sheets
a dusty man walked as dawn through darkness
bending shadows breaking myths
entering time with rhythm 'n' rhyme
as if this world had been his song all along
he knew our tune and sang it clear
broken spirits heard his words
for what he sang they knew was true
but never could music make it—
it wasn't the miracles or text fulfilled
it was the strain that broke from him
as waves of jasmine on summernight
new and familiar, fresh and proverbial
the more they heard the more they yearned
for the country he came from—
those songs, those words, that tune—
it reminded them of the imagined
they could hear it in his air
and breathe it as it left his lips
like calypso sailing them to tropics

movement iv

through the dark while we waited
for something to be done and over
the coals burned into glowing gods
that took transfigured flaming shapes
and quickened our defunct hopes
that black could burst to glory
but morning revealed the night:
the fire was a pyre, a limp pile
a pointless, phoenixless mound
that never could reignite
or fan into furious flame
and nothing could turn back
we were no longer black
my God, my God, we were white!
not the white of autumn cotton
the happy child's teeth and eyes
the collosal clouds mounting skies
this was dead white, dull and dreary
more dreary than the gray
it was pallid parched pale and painted
on signs on walls on halls on faces
on sweaty t–shirts and hospital gowns
it was government white, newspaper white
the scarred white of cemeteries
the layered white on old mansions
the yellowing white on broken fences
lightless white, hopeless white
the eyes of the awful sick
a garbage swarm of maggots –
and who is to blame for this ashen white?
the wind, the darkness, the night?
the spark that lit the ignesecent core?
this ash was beauty brain and fame

but once lit, that's it, the glow devoured
and we came to our hour
the hour we had waited for
to be done and over
so that we could know for sure
what we had waited for

movement v

these gray stones are not dead
they are clouds sliding through night
in shifting shapes metamorphosed by kind winds
transparent and lucid, the nimbus moon
glows through them, orangebright, as they pass –
each had been so solid, so corporeal
with a name and a place and significance
but now they drift lightly over the earth
changing places, faces, and countenance
sometimes thick, sometimes thin, they wing
across the sea's horizon like effulgent cherubim
ablaze with sunburst, aglow with holy morning glory
they migrate to dark mountaintops
where they mingle with the old mists
and draw our seekings upward into hosts
of spirits gathered in cathedraled hues
above those blackbarked birch
bleeding bloodred, purple, yellow
in violent plumes against sable woods

August – November, 1998

46. the moment

there were hundreds before this one
    speeding breakaways past grabbing defenders
quick dribbling shifts and deft left–footers
    wall benders, looping wingers, desperate diving headers
swerving corners, upper–ninety blasted scorchers
    driven past outstretched fingers
tense penalty kicks slid low inside the post
    solo shots and last–minute winners
each scored with sweat, team, and vigor
    all different and some specially remembered
but this one was all of them come true:
    a ranging pass from a thirty–yard cross
came arching ahead of your speeding path –
    losing a marker shadowing your side
sidestepping a sweeper impeding your stride
    seeing the keeper bounding from his line
quickly knowing not to try a header –
    you leaped horizontal as high as your shoulders
and volleyed the ball with one momentous motion
    filling the net and expectation

September 1998

(tribute for John – and for a goal scored in the first game of 1998
season against North Georgia)

47. unexpected, unregretted

this day, my son, has come
unexpected for me, unregretted,
unanticipated and different
an indian summer sneaking up
in numb november
after all the leaves have browned
and fallen frosted to the heavy ground
      I'm flushed with contentment
knowing that the song you hummed
and so very long imagined
now has words and rhyme and magic
(you can't get her out of your head)
she's flesh of your dreams, incarnate wish,
strong to save you from yourself
born to take your loneliness
      so you, my son, must be to her
as she's to you, a prophecy fulfilled
a promise, as old as God, come true
nothing should separate you two
nothing so long and hard and good as life
for when this day ends, night will come
a moth to glowing candlelight
with wings as brown as the long goingdownsun

November 28, 1998

(to Jeremy on his wedding day)

48. those who know you

the pines, the tall straight pines
we saw them bend in hurricanes
and snap back erect
glistening in the fresh sun
after the storm
and we saw them do it again
and again, like you
as if numb to the wind

you have a way of calming
those who know you

the wheel wasn't invented for such as you
nor engines nor modern machines of any kind
you are from the era of the plow
steady, making furrows, for next year's corn
to feed the family
always looking forward
never back
for that would make a crooked line

those who know you
can now see straight

even when you get tired
and droop and sway
like the sprawling oaks giving shade
you are admired
and talked about
if not felt
a glimpse of you is enough – enough
to quench any complaint

those who know you
have nothing to say

the night is quieted by nimbus moon
paddling through a sea of stars
silently on course, in line, on time
not disturbing anything
as it follows straight behind the sun
the crooked stars we call constellations
and celestialize as heroes and gods
but you get the prize – glowing venus

those who know you
have much to praise

the new earth belongs to your kind
the kind that fills ravines
uncrooks the bends in rivers
and flows
the new Jerusalem has gates for you
simple straight and narrow
for we can't imagine
you to ever stray

those who know you
know you're safe

December 24, 1998

(for Nancy, who asked me to read this poem
at her memorial service, which I did in June of 1999)

49. with us still

not yet
no, not yet
still with us, thank God
you're with us still

while deers in the forest moan
deers driven to numb mountains

you are not ghost
still flesh and breath
yet with us, warm,
(bless Immanuel)

the wicked highway, bloodstained
curves around the groans

but angels silence us
angels moving quicker than deers
quieter than light
then disappearing into trees

while one body and only one
lies in the brown grass still

December 30, 1998

(the day after John's accident)

50. cannot change

I see separate days
aging separately
flowering gorgeous
fullbossomed
trimly muscled
bulging with beauty
chiseled and sheen
a glory in the sun
retaining some glow
of happiness
but then it comes
and I see it coming
and cannot change

I see the face but once
and know that he is human
his flesh will peel away
whether male or female
gorgeous or grotesque
the man will be his bones
I see it and cannot change
even when I see the smile
light up the face
that will wrinkle off
and fall away
into a pile of other faces

I see the familiar faces
come and go
as ghosts and photos
on the mantle
I see them failing
and cannot change –

I hate this knowledge
that came from God
knows where
this knowledge
that my fingers
will fall off
with my toes
into a pile of digitals
next to dinosaur's bones
I see it and cannot change

I have tried to stop it
just one hour
to command it
to hold still
but the rebel
aching for air
grasping for touch
hangs anyway
over the water
at owlcreek bridge
the sun bends
the moon follows
the crickets and frogs
holler through the night
I waste in sleep
and cannot change

I couldn't stop it
if I tried
Jesus did once
a dead son
and dying mother
on a funeral march
were made alive

and everyone was happy
until it came again
I saw this coming
and could not change

oh, too many poets
spoke of it
(give it up, Emily
let it go, Edgar)
but they couldn't
even by grace
because this is
what they faced
when they felt
the skin–'n–bone winds
cut through faith
they could not
no, they would not
be anymore –
they saw it coming
and could not change

what use the suffering
the slow degeneration
of bone and brain –
the insanity of the sane
shepherding those
who've lost
their minds
the most determined
will wander
the most faithful
will doubt
when the wheels
begin to fall off

and the hands
can't find the reins
especially when they see
it coming
and cannot change

the man who ran by me
a moment ago
will become thoughts
bones and ghost
I think of him and cringe
he's not the man
I used to be
he's running ahead
too quickly
as though he saw it coming
but cannot change

January – March 1999

51. a well–lit stair

light is precious
a certain lean of light
soft, immaculate, unoppressive
making gentle fall
on the shadows of your eyes –
oh, what radiance in sight:
slow Serengeti sunstreaks
Anarctic cerulean suncast
autumnleaves gleaming
after a storm has fattened and thinned –
isn't the light sweet and good?
as good as God glowing
on flowerflocked snowsmeared Murrin –
it's bright that almost blinds!
but then it bends and turns kindly
leading you round the obscure
and far past the feared
to unsuddenness, a well–lit stair

February 7, 1999

(to my mother)

52. missing you

this day scattered shadows long and thin
and I, alone, was missing you
everyone I called friend
I was missing you
because only you know what we've been
when were innocent
when we were sin
when we were changing the world
then the shadows got thick
they layed down dead and flat
no birds chirped or frogs croaked
and I was missing you
again

February 12, 1999

53.   the drinking gourd

with nothing but sweating sun
laboring to be delivered from dawn till dusk
in the drymouth head–drained heat
in the alligatorsummer scald
scorched of all desire but one
they desperately sing the drinking gourd
and look long to the north
on mosquitoed mississippi nights
swashed in dank swampsmell

"but I can't, no I can't,
though I've tried
to carry the stars
all by myself
across the river"

Abraham had a sackful
flung over his shoulder
but he hardly scattered any seed

"nevermind, I hear yonder
the waves making sands
and the dark pushing out
red foxes and packs of stars
in search of justice"

March 6, 1999

54. errata

I am crumpled
 o
to^ many mistakes

       e
   unforgiveabl^
pronouncing
loudly unabashedly
in front of everyone
that counts
you are error
a mistake creptInto the text
a corrupption
unaware of how much damage it would spell
the misspellingg
was desperately rubbed
blotted
   even crossed out
but they spotted the orignal flaw
the diorthotes
     had to straighten you out
but most–of–all–the–wrong–of–you
   is left there forever
a stupiD letter in the line
an incompetent strok e
  a n e n t i r e s e n t e n c e r u n n i n g o f f t h e p a g e
           past fixed margins
a poor reflction of the exemplar
   you are guilty
of ditography[sic]
   a reperepetition of Many slurs

of haplography

                         you leaped ahead
but you got caught
            in the critics' net—
      the Pluperfect have found you out
and nailed you up
a placard in the scholars' courtyard
to be egged and bookreviewed
              with scorn—FUSTIGATE him!
you are the idiot caught dead in print

with no way out
      but to recant, rescind, remander
take him to the junkyard of bad print
that desperately tried to matter

July 30, 1999

73

55. it is said

he is own heaven
but mostly he is hell
invisible is his darkness
a settled hades beneath his thoughts
he already knows the eschaton   it is lonely
sad are the eyes
that have looked for it to come
in any way spectacular   it is here
roaming his mind
most mornings
stealing simple joys
(everything will burn?)   it is already
too desolate
too determinative
a reversal could hardly be expected
from what he has sensed
of divine rage
unless there is another way   it is fixed
kinder, even kindest is death
for fugitives of fate
(his haunted mind begs repose)
give it, please, crushed creator
if you wouldn't mind tenderness—
kisses are the best   it is said

August 1999

56. winged words

dreamcatcher, you have holes
flaws and tears. everything
I imagined – winged words –
have flown through you
skinny, so thin, insubstantial
I have not been able to catch
or get my hands round
thin sheets. even thinner,
letters flat on the page
are next to nothing

the monarch's wings are fatter
it flies somewhere
migrating to mexican mountains
before the thin winter air,
where it congregates
with myriads of voyagers
in thick orange clusters,
making me believe
there must be a solid heaven
beyond every verb

August 11, 1999

57. Iam

known by the innocent Iam groped for soon enough
when lost to sense Iam chased, pursued
sometimes in a flash Iam seen in books
and caught in anguished looks
      I riverovermountainrocks
can't be snared or sepulchred
IamWavesFetchFrothFoamPelicanStorkGullLoon
Iam seaSpillreefBreakgullSplashrockCrash
tidePushmoonPullfishFlushbirdSwarmwindDraft
      Iam succulentJuice MangoPapayaOrange
Iam undulatingAspen bucklingPine
waterOuzel slippingFall glacierShifting
movingMeadows sinkingFurrows
      Iam divinescent flowerooze sundrink
that brokenopen essence that flick that kick
that slightest touch of monarchlegs
on branchbend in floweryawn
      Iam caw crawl fishspurt grainsprout
bobcatBounding pumaSleekness forestRain
seapeeling earthbreaking sunsoaking lifescent
that earthturned wiff eyeglint joyburstAftersadness
sigh touch of invisibleQuick
      I Spiritmove intoEveryLivingThingIam
I dewdescend on spiders' webs
the diamond crystals in translucentSun
I chamelion green lizardbacks to brown
lighten murkiness Let darkness cloud
      I do not come to reason or defend
but transform U g LY to thin and flat to ROUND
ubiquitous, I cannot flee

nor you me
IamFalconflightWindhold
Iam hermit crab's search for conch
man's dream other planets are not parched
Iam woundedmolluskpreciouspearl
Iam spiritBreathpneumaAir
IamRushFountainWingsMotion
no cistern can hold me square
     I MoveMentoMadness
console bereft in their despairsadness
by unexpected magnoliaBloom
the breaking of exoticScent
heaven's jar unscrewed and poured
     whatever has being has being in me
IamMeaning IamTruth IamYou—
can't you see me in a thousand figures
lovely limbs, uncommon faces
signatured, distinct, unscrolled
each takes its shape from within
and shouts to the glories, IAm
     I will never be endangered though hunted
by all religions who haven't figured
Iam tideSurge windDrop treeFall
mushroomSproutspriggedLeaftreeRot
s t r e a k e d sunset blackcatdarkness
Iam tidechange sucked back over smooth stones
clacking in liquid s w o o s h and waveSurge
     can't you see Iam zoe?
all that ISaliveISalive with me
the peaTendril reaching for staked post
the redFox chasing bald pink sun
the mother milking twins with double tits

I feed all—Iam nutrient never spent
I sustain flesh with spirit—they are lent
until I take them back again.
this is not cruel or fluke or fair
this is what is and what is meant
       this galaxy has not spun forever
but I have always been
nothing could expand to be as Iam
and nothing can diminish me
as the tall grass waves in the wind
don't think it has no thought for me—
freshly mown, smell its sweetSacrifice
so are each of the trillion deaths to me
the squishedAnts scream and hooked fish
(their end is no less human)
      I cannotstop or backlook on what I was
for Iam vineblood humanserum spit and sperm
sap of Marchmaples Rainsoaked sweetcane
chickorycluster poking blue
through speckledgray rockcrack
Iam mountainlava oceancurrent
d o l p h i n g l i d e a n d p l u n g e
seahawk s w o o p ClawandTongue
fishwriggle flash and fetch
      Iam unboxed light exploding atoms
catch a glimpse of the topquarx smashing
but Iam thinner than can be scanned
the space surrounding atoms Iam
and the place that atoms are
      I can crawl into a sandcrab's hole
or blackholes cram with denser light
I can permeate the crooks of mind

coloring them with evil or with right
though I weigh nothing
I sit heavy on the guilty
and refuse to forsake those who curse me—
Iam as faithful to spirit as spirit is to me
    don't think Iam evolution
I journey my biography
for Iam as Iwas and willbe as Iam
I cannot be ForestedFetteredForgotten
Iam aftermilennia afterHaveComeandGone
and the earth has no morsels left to give
Iam amillion mouths at once
underOnAbove the scalloped masses
a sea of leaves revealing this:
the floweringWheat is sure as my lips
for Iam always and always is

1998–1999

58. sounds of sadness

mute moon, dumb sun
you have no message
no bottled plea for help
as you bob in the sky
the last thing I will hear
is stars tumbling into sand –
the prophets' huzzah
sizzles, is muzzled
the land is clogged.
snap the trees
shape them into flutes
long thin mellow lutes
sorry for fattening sorrow
sad for your troubles
in hollow notes
more tubular than your emptiness
and anything you could moan
to the numb sky
fumbling on the keys
for something significant

the hollow flute
says it's searching
for a filling of itself
an ending of the note
as it draws out
our wanderings
from the bottom
of all we've felt
and takes it passed
regrets and loss
to places we haven't yet –
we know it's somewhere

God speaks it
everyonceinawhile
fluent and unforlorn.
mostly we hear the moan
saying life is swift
existence slow
both are causes
for deepness sadness
but not for gloom

what we catch now
in brighter tones
with moment
in each movement
will be gloriously quiet
and suncast smooth –
the long land
will last longer
than itself
and produce fruit
each fresh month
green and red and redder
while we get
never old and tired of it
the slow trees say so
down the long stretch of mind
where dogs prance
the fresh grasses
and harts leap green ferns
farther than you could ever planet

the weak
the meek
the gentle know
the hapless

the hopeless
will shine
because the sun
balling the sky
will not burn up
as long
as there is
Jesus
and the fish
that keep coming
like shells
tossed up from sea
(old bodies
 new shapes)
and the rest will come
the rest will come
I know

spring 2000

59. we sing you on your way

the sea was silver
so was the sky
with a punch of sunshine
breaking through

it would only be time
till you pushed beyond
the cloudsmear and skycast
beyond the bend of trees and wind

time, that taker of love
was moving you more distant
than our hands could touch
(what was it we groped to grasp?)

we, fumbling on this side,
can't feel enough to comprehend
so we sing you on your way –
for song is longer than prayer

a swifter chariot to cherubim
always and forever extolling Christ
chanting holy, holy, holy Lord
holy is your going, Nancy

the clouds are broken open now
sunshine greens the sea
and heats the stretch of beach
where you first scanned the dolphins' leap

we open our hands to these winds
as we let you ocean go to God
and free you to the Spirit
moving and brooding unwatched

May 28, 2000
(Nancy's memorial service; a poem
for the scattering of her ashes)

83

60. And then

1.

Sometimes I have to scream at you
whom some call blessing, others a curse
(that all depends)
you are really nothing yet you have always been
the worst
you make me love each moment too much,
detest the linear.
There they lay long and stiff before their bones
have grown crooked
unposed for the gray photograph clicked still
at Antietam
each must have prayed their eternity. now
we don't know.
Some turned to face you head to head
spit you in the eye
refusing to fear what's called a lie.
others determined
to flee faster than the curse can catch
but you lift the head
strike the heel and drag to dust.
I scorn you for leaving halftones, tawny manuscripts
in broken ink
dried roses, tearstained memoirs, musty basements
cobwebbed attics,
faded stellaes, imperfect cylinder seals, broken shards
of ostraca.
I laugh at you for forcing me to write
(you're no muse)
who'd call on you for inspiration? and yet you spurn –
for no one
I know has beaten you with stylus or chisel.
those epitaphs

must amuse, befuddle, as some scorn
and others resign
to recorded deeds done against the bracket of time.
Sunshine white
the long stretch of crosses say either you're right
or nothing's sovereign.
the music, no matter how fast it's drummed,
cannot overtake you
their songs' yearnings are longer than the bugle
but not longer
than the silence of the unvisited.

2.
the glance of eyes transect
catching each other's thoughts just
long enough to peel away some distance
between what never can be written
        my wife's embrace, too quick to keep
her fingers quickening the keys
the sonata's epiphanic rise and fall
silence steals, remorse saddens
        (I haven't caught the moment)
primed waves pitch, plunge, drop, roll
past a retriever chasing slippery pelicans
winging into the dark dusked sun
        I'd hurl evanescence's preciousness
if I could immutable hold –
or do I yearn for everlasting transcience
the elusive fugitive, God?
        nonlinear, unchronicled, the push to places
of the mind, the near fulfillment of dreams
grasped, lapsed, words come true, not truer
all language explored, exhausted, spirit

3.

creamwhite magnolia blossoms crushed in the palm.
the fragant flash. sweet. gone.
dreams gripped in dark slipping through the crack of dawn
suns you swear you saw
oceans you slid into and out dripping with God.
there is sadness in the taking,
a lack of movement to the celestial wheels
rotating, girating. the goggling
of seven eyes of seven spirits watching the wicked
wear this world. (enough.)
I'm tired of running for rest. There must, there has
to be a page after the book
a sound after cymbal's crash, another explanation
than there's nothing
mindful after us. Yes, I've heard owlhoot, frogcroak,
dogbark, dovesong
say nothing significant and say it all—it doesn't end
with bang or whimper.
it just doesn't end. never mind the long explanations.
short is best and sweet.
we're gonna live forever because we think
in the long swoop of God
and arch of angels there's a hallowed peace of earth
primed for children
laughing innocent and pure, seeing him invisible
visage of us all. And then

May, 2001

61. Ancient Egyptian Exhibit

though he could keep his name hidden
from his chest, he lifts his signet
with precious image of his hupostasis and
creature likenesses, then rolls the wet marl
with cachets of his distinguished signs
    genuine impressions, rare expressions
carved grooved indented raised
a rolled–out pictograph, projecting reliefs
in long stretches of proof and space
    falconwings flash his span from here to star
talons his hold, seven eyes his omnivision,
puma his sleekness, phoenix his fetch from ash
an array of zoatics, aquatics, aerials
are zodiacs of the imprinting wheel.
    soMuchmore this one has yet to spin
the universe is still stretching space
the galaxies widening into galleries
to hold this poet's craft, to catch the spirit's drift
    of the invisible yearning immanence,
the incorporeal lusting even lumps of flesh
moist clay, thin drawn strips of it
nearly insubstantial, vastly water
to press to solemn significance
    one symbol after another rising
each emblems of his majesty, dignity, grace
imprints of the Logos. faces of GodgoneHuman
emerging from limpness, dampness, void
    each his artifice, his autographic poem
no matter how they wrinkle or go terribly worn
the indiscernible is scrutable, decipherable
in terrestial shapes as the genius rotates
and envisioned images swell real. flashed. fixed

July, 2001

62. until kingdomCome

until kingdomCome
men will fight over whose God is right –
they will martyr for The Cause.
until kingdomCome
and Truth is personally revealed,
they will grip their holy books and cry
"we're the rightful heirs of paradise!"
until kingdomCome
and the Righteous One appears
with glory beyond dumbfounding words
men will bend prayers hoping God knows
they're bedeviled by goddamn infidels.
until kingdomCome
and God's Son outshines luciferous glow
more effulgent than conflagrant stars
men will say prophetic voices
have made them furiously right
to execrate this earth of godlessness.
until kingdomCome
the meek hide in prayer and disecretely
move between this world and next
smuggling with them secrets of the light
and answers to the dark, while they watch
and implore the LordofAll Jesus Christ
to split the skies and kingdomCome.

October 2001

63. we saw his face

the other side is too narrow to squeeze
too big to flatten, too fluid to grasp
(angels mingling wind, waves becoming froth)
we are too lost on this side to know
too fragile to face Glory head on
for fear we'll be squashed and ruined
and love can't push us beyond

yet as flesh wanes thin, the fatter eternity looks
the better we know ourselves and desperateness
for grace to come, "o Lord," we moan, "yet don't –
I am not ready, never worthy, never better
(do you care?) or does love thrust you through
our gnarled souls to take us in our weakness
and make us transparently unknowingly like you?"

in the quiet of anguish, in the search of soul
we saw his face in David's, we touched effulgent grace.
these things can be said only of those who've known
their dying is the dying of their Jesus
their living is the living of their Christ.
there is no end for the Savior's friends
(look! the beginning is just now breaking open)

the new earth doesn't have days that end –
it is heaven. expected. gloriously green and new.
we will meet there and sing fresh songs
in strong sunlight gathered in God's smile
and yes, we will cry, but not for sadness
because Jesus, the giver of all things good,
not its taker, wipes every tear from our eyes

November 8, 2001   (in memorium for David Godby)

89

64. figure chaos

daevas thickened the swirling kosmos
mixed myriads populating the invisible
evil spirits mingled with good
in mooncast sundown darklight
shadows bright with jinn and shen
spiriting everywhere nowhere known
daimonia deities pleroma manas
gods who created then took off
with other names to other kingdoms
while we were left to figure chaos

that's why prophets came, they said

Zarathustra spake "the gods are dead"
only Ahura Mazda is LordAllWise
author of evil maker of good
sainted Satan ambivalent God.
Moses proclaimed the IAMwhoIAM
YaHWeH EverExistingOne.
others abandoned the heavens
(strange to the spot were in)
Mahavira beat his karma to death
attaining moksha, sweet release.
Siddhartha saw flesh, couldn't starve
desire, craved truth, drank nirvana.
Lao–tzu found Tao, the sacred flow
while wise Confucius said nothing new

these all discovered hades themselves

then another came, not to explain
demons devotions pangs and trouble
but to face the human loathe with love,
not to raise apothegm from the crypt
but to create. This was healer of longsick
curer of sin–death, paintaker, paradiser,
pioneer of the tenebrous curse
who said he was himself the Way
then journeyed beyond the graves

summer 2001

65. surfer

the sea is glass, a pond to skate on
a mirror for the sky's changing faces.
young tanned men come and go to shore
with strapped boards and fixed memories
but tide after watched tide drops their mood
like the half–lit moon in the west
but so does the pressure
        the ground slowly swells beneath the sea
bumping up substantial successive ridges
a southwestern holds them firm and strong
as they move along, rising higher and thicker
until they peak and trim a hundred yards long
each wave peeling off, dropping, pearling
as if some invisible finger slid down an ivory keyboard
        but the sound is not piano – it's percussion
tight snare roll, zildjian crash, morocco sizzle
as the surf breaks and stallions toward shore
past darting mullet and skimpering sandpipers
to the ankles of these bronzed islanders
bound to the sea and the board that takes them
beyond the chop, breakers, and roll
        where they watch the culmination
of arduous African migration
storm–swelled over far fetches
wall after liquid wall moves toward shore
as the surfers take off in fierce anticipation
of the thrill of standing under that curl
that can thrust or crush the interloper
who dares to call himself surfer

fall 2002

Pawleys Island, South Carolina
(for my son Peter)

92

66. not going yet. crazy

why don't you, gracious presence, stay, intensify –
more than moon grow fuller in my night's sky
or sneek indian summer before the brittle fall?
this invisible flow, this Spirit of your person
becomes to me and surrounds me in epiphany
as when you broke the tomb. but no show of face.
my dead body will release you and God will run
wilder than prophets' dreams. to see you as you are.
(too hard for me, a spit of flesh, to comprehend)
yet I have nothing else to hang on – only the wind
bending trees and your Spirit hovering in mine,
moving, sweetening dread time, loving me deeply
for no good reason, giving me grace for mistakes,
grace for aging, grace for not going yet. crazy.

October 12, 2002

67. leaf dances

early november. cold enough to worry
warm enough not to care as the sun
breaks through the graying clouds and I sit
legs spread out in the fallen leaves
with my grandson on a going–nowhere
sunday afternoon. I twirl one of the fallen
mangled brown elms. "Look, it twirls,"
I show him. He grabs it and says, "leaf dances!"
as he moves the stiff stem between his slim
finger and thumb. "Leaf dances! Leaf turns!
Leaf spins!" he giggles. One leaf after another
he danced. "Yellow leaf dances. Red leaf dances.
Brown spins." We laughed and threw leaves
on each other's heads and watched the sun fall down.

November 3, 2002

(for Reid, my three–year old grandson)

68.   the beach is his

the beach is his. he makes it. the darting minnows
    in surge, suck, sally. the sandpipers scurrying
    between swooshes. the dallies with clawing crabs.
the pelicans bobbing on the sea like sun.
the swim, the search in crushed waves for the stick I pitched.
the fetch, prance, strut – like a majorette, he waves the stick
    as high in the air as he can get it.
        he is good so good. the universe is his.
those who stroll by sense, catch, smile, and share the glow
    as we kick our way through the shallows
northwardheaded – I with board in hand and he with stick in jaw
    and slosh our way to the northern spit
where I begin to surf nor'eastern shifts and slide winddown
    southbound breaking lefts, all the while trailed
by my companion who watches my catches and follows my drift
excited by every ride, he runs along, my terrestial shadow.
and even if I mingle with a swarm of other blackgarbed surfers
    he stays fixed on me until I ride the last wave to shore
where I am met in the shallows by the sweetest soul
    with dance, swagger, primal joy, contagious happiness.
he wants more. so much more. never to leave the surging sea—
to chase dogs, rays, and falcons, to fetch, catch anything called life
    but I exhausted soaked and spent, coax him toward the exit,
where we pass many a local who don't known my name
nor I theirs, but they call out anyway: "Charlie! how's the surf?"

November 2002

(for Charlie, my golden retriever)

95

69. dogangel

living on water and air and my love
I thought you'd make it to the warm days –
how you craved the sun as your body thinned
you still flared your nostrils to the wind
but couldn't chase. there was no more prance
left in you, though you wanted to please.

the last good day together we shared the beach
and winter sun with two families of dolphins
no more than a paddle away. they lit the ocean,
leaped, flipped, danced, dallied, pranced, played.
I know, Charlie, I know how you wanted to join –
you waded the frigid surf but couldn't swim.

the last grim days dragged slow as old January
and I spoke nothing significant and couldn't change
the end, as we watched one cold sunset after another
die and I clung to keep the spirit of us alive
but I couldn't keep you from going to ghost –
I read it in your desperately sweet brown eyes.

the moment you left I went weeping to the drenched sea
I passed some children throwing bread and laughing
as a swarm of cawing seagulls circled overhead.
then they shouted with delight into the cold mist:
"look, dolphins!" and I saw the twins streaming silver,
sea's angels, as sure of where they headed as eternity

January 31, 2003

(the day a glorious soul of a golden retriever named Charlie
left this earth and went to the next)

70. they see and cannot say

ah, the mouth is vile. the tongue lump.
they cannot speak what they have seen.

dying men dying visions. the last flash
slides, slips through, lost in gaping lacuna

before it's mouthed. Mohammed didn't come.
Nor an angel. Nor a host of saints dropping heaven.

Jesus speaks. The Spirit says. Living creatures
whirl around the throne, moan, praise, kneel, rise,

eye the celestial Lamb still bleeding, feeding
manna to mouths, light to darkness, liquid words

dripping God. In and out. But they can't articulate.
It is all like. All like. A simile. A metaphor. A poem

spun like heaven from one end of everlasting
to the other. And no one this side of vision can say.

They break through skies but can't push the image out.
They collapse into sprawl, scrawl, limp, lanky lines

on leaves, ostraca, papyrus, skins, bones, and paper.
Anything thin. But the vision is too big. Too animal

to capture. Too fluid. Too spirit to set between
the edges of paper. To spell. To lay flat and dead.

The print cannot rise. The voice lifts. The spirit.
The flute. The throated longings. Breath blown

into a reed. Somewhere in there the vision voices.
Somewhere in there the poet sees what can't be said.

The restless have to speak. The rested don't. While
the rest await the word. They wait the Lord. The long

strong dreams keep all else asleep. When they wake
they know they've seen but cannot say. Apocalypse

comes in waves. And goes. And is. And was.
And is to come what is and was. An everlasting

sound from heaven. An ocean on another shore.
They were there and heard it, they say. I hear

the waves pounding my coast. Beating the beach.
The heave, flop, crash. The swoosh, slosh, sizzle.

No human glows. I know. The words can't overflow
the parchment. Caught as we are between the waves.

March 7, 2003

71. fresh fields fill your hands

though dusk has crawled into the horizon
we do not believe the light has fallen
the sun is going home

though wetness wraps round this globe
we do not believe that sea is lord
the earth will rise again

love, it is said, is stronger than death, longer than life
love, it is felt, is the sweetness of Christ broken open

the seeds you planted are sprouting children
each with your face, each with your faith
that fresh fields fill your hands

the skies you remembered mounting Nebraska
yield to sunlight painting paperthin clouds
coloring the air with laughter

love, it is known, is stronger than death, longer than life
love, it is felt, is the Spirit of Christ never leaving us alone

for Jim Ellermeir, my good neighbor and friend
June 2003

72. gone to spirit

I can't bear to look at your pictures. I'm sorry
I have moved you around the house.
Is that you by my side? Then why this ache?

Yet I see you everywhere. In the blue heron
with arched neck. In the golden eyes of the bright egret.
I call them you but they fly away when I bone near.

I thought I saw you on the bridge, but it was another
I couldn't name. I called you anyway. I spoke you
into wind hoping that would make you appear.

Everywhere I look I remember where you were
and what we did. Strangest was when I dug up some dirt
and saw you wriggle in the worm. Is this insane?

I reach up into sky, grasp, and want to flow naked like you
but you fly through like clouds like water. I cannot hold.
I know you've gone to spirit, but I have ghosted into air.

August 2003

73. your questions now answered

when a forest of fires rages and cuts down pinnacles
we trusted to stay mountain high, what is it that will seed?
when knees go numb and words stumble in confusion
falling over themselves into ruin, what is it that can be said
to those you loved: your precious wife, sons, daughters;
your beloved students, your dogs who warmed your feet;
your universal contemplations, the philosophic twist of phrase?
will your questions now answered by the risen Lord who saves?

we know that death doesn't hang. sorrows cannot conquer.
immortality is not illusion, for there isn't end to those who grave.
new earth now erupts more beauteous than Estes Park
and fecund heavens will unfold scrolls of unraveled texts.
you will read, as you have been read—long before prophets spoke
and Jesus said, "I am the resurrection of the living and the dead."

September 16, 2003, for my uncle John Comfort (1928-2003)
a poem read by my father, Richard Comfort, at John's memorial service

74. God's claws

I wasn't ever told God had claws. I didn't know
until he scraped long furrows where I haven't ever been.
Or in a long time. He clawed his way into some
longforgotten cistern.
      It sputters. Spouts. Gushes. Flows uncontroled
into too many tears. Grace drips from his mouth,
while his talons still scrape, digging into darkness.
O God, uncover light!
      What is it that makes your hand so heavy?
My head hurts. My heart. My soul.
But I don't know who turn to except you who claws.
I have lost sense.
      I want to lose this darkness. Long unbroken darkness,
long unbroken darkness. Is it Satan who has come?
There is no deception of light.
There is no light.
      Lord Lion Christ, maul me. Quick break.
If it must be, let me be ripped with some
substantial kindness. I'd rather split
into brightness than escape.

October 2003

101

75. heavy dirt

I'm under a ton of dirt, heavy dirt.
Usually I'd want to dig my way out
to kick and squirm, maybe scream
at the universe for falling on me.

I was just walking along small, minding
my own life when something bigger than me
grabbed me and threw me into a deep pit,
covered it and walked away without a word.

Usually I'd conjure up a way out.
Think good thoughts. Talk resurrection
and stuff. Hope for someone to come along
with a shovel. Pray deeply. Meditate.
Contemplate why the earth is so heavy.

But here I am laying flat. In the dark
with no leg room. Strange. I don't mind.
There's no one here to point out
my immurement. To take a picture. It's quiet
enough to hear my own measured breathing,
to feel heart and blood pulsing my veins.

I'm just under a ton of dirt, that's all,
waiting in this orb until one day,
I know, it will blow up. And I, freed spirit,
will spin and loop, swirl and sizzle.

October 2003

76. aura

An epiphany of stars signs our insignificance
        each evening. it happens.
the sky falls off and dogs into haze
(another page ripped off the book)
        I prefer the unloneliness of day
one sun in the sky. light and easiness.
night is for sleeping. making fires.
gazing into embers. not looking up
where wings and lost thoughts ghost
the dark giffin-like, where ancient mariners
in caravans cruise celestial spheres
searching for other Jerusalems, I guess.

Against unmastered dark,
        clouds spirit past paper flim
thinner than sky, thinner than skin
        translucent with moonshine
                bursts and flashes of it
as fatter spirits bloat and bleed
move as wind into wind
between us and the uncut beyond
the facelessness of space
lost in stars, masses of nameless stars
birthing and dying, bright then black.
        in moving wind clouds transfigure and figure.
        and I imagine
            meaning breaking through and going long
in the long march of clouds,
        the souls of God, fleeting creatures
        seeking light to break their glory on.

I like light. shafts of it. casting shades and
shadows long and bare. openess between trees.
leaves sucking air. illuminated dirt.
I'm edgy with cities lit up with headlights
weaving through murkiness and lamplights
laboring to heave off heavy darkness.
it cannot be shoveled away
as if it were snow or sand. only dawn exorcises.
ah brightness! handfulls. bucketfulls. barrelfulls.

I cannot imagine more lucid glory
than what surrounds. clouds mingle with sun
light with wind stretching greens into glistening shades
and blue is so pleasant to the sky.
I am spirited with these lights, these lives.

what red is thicker than the woodpecker's hood—
what flash of orange than oriole's wing?
no gold is purer than the snowy egret's iris.

so fluid, fair, unpretentious, stems of light
shoot through leaves in peregrine plunge,
falcon spiral, seahawk dive, heron bob.
light arches, curves, and heaven heaves.

Light is sweet. stems of it. blazed. uncolored
undying, unstruggling, not having to breathe.
it's wind I've never seen bending round long objections
it travels seas, traverses minds, and always returns
pure, untired. untainted, its aura inheres, inspires.
never the-dark-no-exit. but the unexpected exodus—
the journey so sweet, so gracious, so for the making.

the light is face, God's face. God's mouth. coming out.

When light leaves the eyes like an old man
        trying to get out his house for the last time
                on cane on crutches on anything but help
                on longings for winterless woods where
streams of sunshine green everylivingthing--
        when this light creeps out from behind the eyes
the spirit goes with it slowly, at first, like a cat
testing the ground with its front paws,
like a dog sniffing the wind for wild scent,
        but then it knows it's right to wend, to leap
                not into the grim unknown but to its own
                        sacred air and breath and break of glory.

I've seen the light fade in faces only to return
for one brilliant blast as when a cloudcast day
turns gloriously sudden at sunset's end.
Some have patina. others lustre. aureole is so hard
to grasp. luminosity harder to sustain.

autumn 2003

77. strange exodus

I cling to this thin flim of touch, this almost-other-worldliness
slighter, finer than brushing into the spider's web at dark,
than fly legs pattering on my skin, than sunlight just breaking
from behind a dark cloud onto the back of my neck.
This thin membrane between one kingdom and the next
I almost break but I'm too firm a flesh.
Wings couldn't get me through. Even water has weight.
If I got lank and lean, angel slim, I think I could sneak in.
But I must emaciate. Fall apart. Crumble into spirit
and ghost my way into the invisible strange exodus.

autumn 2003

78. they sang our souls to heaven

After the chorale, some of them went with us
    to a home of broken folk waiting for glory
to break the dread of another day he didn't come
    or they didn't quickly go to him.
It's hard to believe the singers still had breath in them,
    that they could make their throats aeolian.
But their spirits rose like angels with voices
    lifting us to strange unearthly heights—

these men of the chorale who sang our souls to heaven.

It's those looks! those transparent souls we saw that night
    through bodies as thin as moments between here
and next: the souls we glimpsed gushing out their eyes,
    mouths open wide, gaping at the face of Jesus!
This took me by surprise: their swift release through song
    into God's beyond, penetrating despair by airs
of sound becoming brightness. How is it that ordinary words
    became exotic arms lifting them to sacred spaces

as the men of the chorale sang their souls to heaven.

We will all split apart after the last cymbals' crash
    and the final taps desert our nights for lights,
the everlasting lights unrolled like tenorous
    voices not needing to ever steal a breath
but always holding the note, the savored note
    that doesn't end but always sends us farther
and deeper into the cheerful Father of us all
    whose kingdom is just a vault away,

when the men of the chorale sing our souls to heaven.

When each of us edges the exodus,
　　　　let those voices come cherubim to get us,
let those voices fetch our heavy hearts and lift us high
　　　　into choirs of myriad admirers chanting praise
to him who gives air to every saint and spring
　　　　to raise our voices, to lilt with newborn
tongue the mysteries of our transcendence
　　　　in quickened cadence that carries heaven.

November 2003
when members of the US Army chorale sang for Bill Haubrich,
a few months prior to his passing

79.　pull

Dragging the sky behind with draught horse pull,
　　　　it lugs people out of bed, plants out of soil,
　　　　　　and stars out of hiding, lunar-powered
　　　　it heaves heavy waters from chasm to shoal.

　　　　It's no mystery I feel wrested and tugged
toward some predestined shore,
　　　　a sled hooked to an invisible invincible Animal
that keeps pulling me unrelentlessly—
I know not upward, outward, or downward.

　　　　I keep groping inward thinking there's
　　　　a hitch but since I don't ever feel I've grasped it
I grip its tethers for the ride of my life
　　　　as I am dragged to God only knows where.

January 2004

80. fugitive

When we think our prince has run fugitive,
       self-exiled from his dominion,
avowed a priest in cloistered heaven,
       abandoning this world to those who crave
the Godforsaken curse, leaving us to vie
       with devils, flesh, and fierce temptation,
we call on him to rend reverence and split heaven:
"Reveal your awful face! Even if it's grim!"

Yet while we moan, supplicate, wonder
       the Parousia, he comes disguised
in those who shore the soul of God
       (epiphanic to the self-absorbed and spent).
These spirits are not us, we sense
       another mind makes their thoughts--
for they do not anguish desperate ends.
       They do not anguish gloom at all.

Sometimes, as the sun is dropping dead
       and dread falls funerary on my hopes
I realize you're one of them again
       and I'm caught for what I haven't been.

January 2004
for Georgia

81. when I came here as spirit

When I came here as spirit from Spirit,
        a wave pushed from sea, I didn't know I was
once immortal channeled into mortality.

I must have liked it where I was before,
        roaming with spirited angels. Undying. Free.
But God must think divinity is lost without faces

in whom to live and breathe his being.
        Could it be that my life is his because it really is—
that as I am not apart from him, so he without me?

I know that when my lover and I touch,
        it is the palpable catch of beings
once unembodied now grasping sense.

It's the mortal parting I don't get—that we will disappear
        as our spirit unfleshes and wriggles out
from this tired space and crowded bones.

Slit an opening in eternity and slide out before anyone sees
        I am there as I have always been—
waiting only for my body to give me up. Quick.

March 2004

82. we have yet to see the face

they clutch the penetrated shroud
       cling to splinters of accacia wood
walk the dolorosa, dip themselves in Jordan
       imagine a holy grail, make quests
through words and words and words
       of those who saw they say visions

others shovel holy dirt, uncover forever
       spade the Nazareth banishment decree,
the ossuary of Caiphas, the ossuary
       of James his brother, the fishermen's boat
sunk in Galilee's muddy waters,
       Bethsaida's pool with seven porches for the sick

others rob monks' graves and caves,
       digging rubbish mounds and church's rubble,
yanking codices stuffed in vases into sunlight,
       pilfering papyrus sheets pressed in piles
of words and words and words of what they said
       in lines and letters bled together

I've deciphered these words, bridged lacunae,
       traced the decorated rounded hand,
biblical uncial, severe and ligatured strokes.
       I've watched the nomina sacra rise off
the page and wander into ancient mouths
       and out again through pilgrim thoughts

I have gotten so close and felt.
       a sprig blown by the wind, I waver
somewhere between faith and next.
       a cenotaph is not enough for me
I hold the mystic spirit, but can't contain--
       it spills and flows into water like wind

110

raised from the dead, they said. taken up.
    all the sagging rows of crosses, all the mute
monuments await the word. but there is never
    enough wind to sweep away the tired from earth.
if he were not gone to ghost, oh spirit,
    we'd have nothing but promise to hold

they preach, they teach, they prophecy.
    mouths move mightily. songs ascend gloom.
they dance, transcend, shout hallelujah.
    chew eucharist with humble teeth. eat host
and pray he stays them another day
    while they dig for more sacredness

his spirit is not enough of, the presence of,
    the sense of, another, immortal, different
than ourselves, who's gone some distance
    yet not left us hopelessly groping to find.
the palpable face flashes. grasp grace
    and cling. squeeze divinity as it passes.

spring 2004

83. I am not the first or last

I am not the first or last to see or know this—
the texts have said it all along, as does the human spirit,
the flower as it blooms, the worm transformed to monarch,
the mother nursing her babe, the father playing catch
with his son, the band who just found the groove,
the poet who finally caught his voice, and two lovers
taking in venus. All too soon. All too soon.

I am not the first or last to see or say this—
the flute has said it all along, as does the last kiss goodnight,
the flower before it falls, the monarch winging south,
the babe grown into child, the father watching his son
slip into manhood, the band that now is music,
the poem that slides from others' tongues, and two lovers
taking in the sun. All becomes. All becomes.

I am not the first or last to say or pray this—
the saints have said it all along, as does the flight to God,
the flower as it seeds, the monarch clinging trees,
the child become a father, the father embracing
his son's children, the band that turned a legend,
the poet who need not prophesy, and two lovers
taking in the moon. All too soon. All too soon.

summer 2004

84. I cannot take it all at once

that there are universes apart from this
          stuffed with plethoric invisibleness
angels, zillions of them, thin as light
          spirits ghosting into hosts of nothing
and all of us here piling up fatter
(imagine earth with everyone living as long as sin)

but where do all the souls go
          those murdered for good
          those who killed sorrows
          and those who leaped light
do they wander to some novae birthing stars?

somewhere between intangible and thrust
        there is no waiting for the caravan to come
no imagining but becoming the imagined
        somewhere between the cracks of dawn
and dusk I rush back into the mouth of God
        and come out singing there is sense

autumn 2004

85. off the edge

ragged is the moon the edge the dropoff
        into whatever that is   the linear lies
the circular the round the bend unchartered
        I frontier thee on edge
by faith against an end

        unhorizontal the fixed   break take down in water
crook the straight bend it into bows
        curling waves oval suns eyeballs sound
round every even thing
    I mean warp the long straight rod
defunct the period
        snap the bracket erase elipses kill end rhyme
        time is not my murderer anymore
ovoid Lord

        I coil spin twist even if I tangle it is superior
        the arc of arch the bow of bend never the end
of hollowing the hallowed
all is rolled
        as I vault the void and sphere into near by far

summer 2004

86. memories of trees

After cloudbreak sunshower, through dancing light I walk
in wet sunshine, make quiet turnings, and pause among
memories of the trees. These who have witnessed
a thousand suns and moons are lights. I walk by them.
I share their earth and oxygen.

These nude trees are not ashamed to show living limbs
caressing their dead. They form a bent canopy to fallen rotting
logs spotted with fungus and mushrooms. Other decaying
beams bridge a brook I step. Here and there new sprigs
sprout from stumps and broken stone.

They have grown long without us and will verve till earth
and sky part. They are their own universe apart, their own
move and mover. As I step small between the angel oaks
and towering pines, I know my age is lost, but they, my host,
feed me mana much as light.

They are books, stories high, epic long, primed, ringed,
totems of red fox hunting, whitetail deer roaming,
Chicora searching the slender moment between sleep
and sound. Moth's wing soft touch, hurricane's brute bend
they've felt and are not stone.

They've spread their aquiline branches to beasts and men
and seen the human unmaking, the undying crimes, the rape
of earth beyond primal recognition. They have jermiads
to moan, as I roam between spiraling shelves and live oaks
and smell their flesh speaking.

Pointing to sky, painting it, they are my higher. They are life.
They did not kill the Christ. They are genesis rising from chaos,
from hardness and crisis. They were spoken and are speaking.
Singing, chanting, exuding. I juice from them, muse them.
I imbibe their foliation.

Their journey is marked in story stick, whether gnarled or straight.
They have been all darkness. They have been all light. They are
earth's sea in the wind, heaving off sadness. Rooted among them
I grow words and throw them into hope like so many branches
stretching for the tall sky.

Slim language for weighty sighs that I carry in sorry old sacks.
The birds don't want my crumbs. They've got wings to climb trees,
while I've got songs. Long songs grasping for something pinnacle.
And thin. Permeable are the leaves of meaning. Breathing still,
the trees have so long to tell.

I bend around the gnarled stippled elms, as the splotched sun
plops oblong behind the treeline break, and I admire the fall.
I stop to count the rings of rememberance and hear their witness
to many suns squating on their long thinning horizons
birthing a forestfull of stars.

summer 2004

87. saving drowning insects

I have a ritual summer mornings:
I try to save drowning insects.

I scoop out bloated cockroaches,
mosquitoes thin as nothing, dreaded horseflies,
scads of no-see-ums, southerners' perennial enemies,
now defanged, undangerous, limp as wet tissue.
I ponder the paradox of intelligent design
(why are those intricately made so irritating?)
as I palm brown moths and toss them over the side,
I wonder why I've never seen a butterfly drown.
They're angels of the insect world I conclude,
as I continue to be more funerary than salvatory.

I accumulate a cadre of corpses:
dragonflies, through whose translucent wings
     I see sun, stingless hornets and flat wasps—
and on occasion I cradle an ephemeral mantis
         fixed in its formidable preying stance.

None of these make it, unless I'm quick.
So who is it that I save?
Bumble bees who can swim for limited minute.
Crickets, black and green, who walk water.
Flying ants who last an hour or even more:
     I've swooped them from the drowning waters
     and set them on the ledge to watch their
     resuscitation, as if they'd been trained--
     blowing miniscule bubbles out their mouths
     flexing their soaked diaphanous wings
     flapping them furiously until they stiffen
     and lift their resurrected bodies in flight
     to make summer another day longer than fate.

The greener-than-grass frogs hiding
in pool cracks eye this rescue with suspicion
hoping mother night will fell them manna
more than they could ever pray to eat

summer 2004

88. American ancestral passage

How many have come to the oceanfront before?
    How many after?--to gaze and contemplate
the waves that keep surging, rolling, lunging, plunging
    long after the long look, that longing look
for someone to break through the crimped horizon
    who saw our forefather standing on this shore
assuring himself of his exodus and an everlastingness
    as long as the waves that keep breaking
in the aura of seabreeze, zephyr, rise, hurl, and buckle,
    plunge, spill, sizzle, pull, and surge.

Maybe this one will tell me what Robert Comfort
    mused when he first arrived on the *America* in 1690
and wobbled on the Atlantic shore squinting at all the sea
    between him and England, between him and his God,
in the waves mounting, cresting, crashing, folding--
    what could he have thought of his pilgrim crossing?
the unfished coast, uninhabited, unclaimed, unboundaried
    except for the fluctuating brink of deep water
that never reaches farther than the finger of God
    even when it fetches, plunges, rushes onto land?

We're told Robert went inland to Fishkill, then Newton,
    parting ways with his two sojourning brothers.
I don't know if his sons, grandsons, and their children
    returned to peer and wonder, to measure the brink,
to ask how far to paradise and how long to shore.
    We're told Robert's son Benjamin kept his home
in the hills of Newton plying his father's tailor trade,
    and that his son John was American in revolution
ripping freedom for us from England's dominical grip,
    to worship God as he saw what fit the truth.

I've seen John's hand that wrote "*in 1794, the eighteenth year*
of independence, I give this last will and testament
before my body returns to dust from which it was taken
and my immortal soul to my God in the humble hope
of a joyful resurrection at the appointed time through the merits
and mediation of my Lord and Savior, Jesus Christ."
As I read this script, my spirit jumped, for I could write
nothing more or hope for anything less.

John passed on the next year and left his sons liberated
soil in the fertile Hudson near Montgomery.
Daniel, the youngest son, journeyed to Ohio, then returned
to inherit 145 acres for farming and raising cattle.
His fourteenth child, also Daniel, had cattle grazing 8,000 acres
under the rolling sun and fecund moon.

In the pages of the Comfort genealogies I've learned
that Daniel's son Walter, with his brother Harvey,
were entreprenurial dairymen, pioneers of icecream
so rich that Walter bought myriad sunsoaked everglades.
His son, I myself knew--my grandfather Harold Comfort,
famed president of Borden's Milk and Elsie's creator.

I don't know if these returned to this shore to trace
the horizon bending 'round them like God's eye,
or if they stood silent as the sun to catch the rising of the sea
and its fall in ebb and flux, rush and roll, bend and break.
I don't know if they grasped why providence had pushed them
from that coast to this. The ocean doesn't easily answer.

The eighth generation Comfort is my father Richard
brother to Hal, Robert, and John;
husband of Dorothy who together made three sons
one who traverses the sea's other side
another who abides in America's heartland
and I who now stand on this Atlantic shore

admiring another sunrise, mystified by oceans of comings
  and goings, by successive generations of waves
still trying to say what Rich, Greg, and I, ninth-generation
  Comforts, have found of freedom or lost.

The ocean never waves out of wonder, winds out of awe,
  nor does the Spirit of life presencing Jesus
from kin to kin—the same Spirit that rolled to my father
  out of the blue and into me like resurrection—
I, who now walk the sea and watch pelicans shoot the curls,
  look for the tenth generation to step on this shore
and discover their sanguinity in this pilgrim water,
  clairvoyant of destiny. This is my prayer for my sons
Jeremy, John, Peter; and for Greg, Bethany, Allison, Bradley:
  "may they sense the eternity God put in their hearts."

My heart brims over when I see awe in the eyes
  of generation eleven. Georgia and I will never forget
how Reid's visage gleamed the first moment he faced
  the waves and seabreeze flushed his cheeks--
so also Drake when he connected with his creator God
  in naked laughter that says it quicker than any poem,
and newborn Jonah, the youngest Comfort, who breathes
  miracles that make us smile and gleam.

May each of us catch the nascent beam, Yah's radiance
  sparkling in children's laughter, pure, pristine,
just right for drinking. May the aureole glow our countenance
  in praise of him who fathers light and life
from one generation to another, born in those who've gone
  before, guiding us all to the other shore.

July 4, 2004 in celebration of the 80th birthday of my father,
Richard Comfort, and previous Comforts

89. for J.D.

though I keep your letters, memories, and laughter
like shells from scattered beaches, you are missed—
you who transported Jesus in such brilliant passages
across oceans to west and east, a Scotsman on a mission
to make us laugh at the unseriousness of ourselves.
every thought of you dawns a smile on my lips,
which is hard to confess about most, even those
who've graced this earth. you were my "daymaker."

when large words leaped from your ink pool
you sent me fishing the dictionary to catch the sense,
while you claimed I sent you romping to orthodox tomes
in gleeful hunt of some wild heresy, hoping to snag me again
in some insidious sacrilege I slipped into the text.
so I was most cautious when you chided,
"no man has a pure heart who cannot spell Habakkuk—
the theological implications of this remark are unthinkable."

your visits from Scotland (not England, may God curse James)
were always a trip (if you'd been a hippie, you'd understand).
you claimed Guy Fawke's day every other month,
signing the ledger you'd come to see Lucille and whispered
"let them talk"—and this from the lips of one who said
  "you can't leap from Delilah's lap into Abraham's bosom—
we unclaimed treasures know such things."

lest I say anything amiss, I confess I was warned,
"he who scoffs at a Scotsman will not prosper."
I have to be careful with one who claimed "certain
throwaway utterances of mine are now common currency."

I laughed with you at your accumulated grievances
that would make any grievance-bearer green with envy—
you who loved to say, "it would have garred ye grue
to see how I glowed in the sheer tawdery of it all"
when you rehearsed your latest injustice with mirth

I loved the impish smile that snuck out your lips
when you threatened the entire evangelical world
with the revelatory disclosings of your memoirs
which might as well be titled, "I know things"—
that you did, but never enough to not know yourself,
and this was Christ's gift you gave us best.

autumn 2004
for J. D. Douglas, my dear friend and co-editor of many volumes

90. excarnate

Sunlight pierce my bones.
deep sunlight. heal.

I am wonderfully made?
Then why unWonderfullyUnMakeMe?

I keep seeking sunlight
somewhere, kinder entropy

Ending is natural consequence
of your choice to make matter—
and to make matter worse
you give intimations beyond bone and lips

Unless this eternity in our hearts is Not—
but if I'm not mistaken,
when we come undone
we will run out of body

exit flesh before I wreck: there's an idea
too Old
          or earth a stint that thins flesh
until it becomes pervious—
excarnate in preliminary lams
          going Zoa-winged. angel it. almost.
each dally rush waveIntoWater
escaped flame from sunfire
U N b o d y part after part

I have too much knowledge: it Hurts

aching for sunlight to melt
thirsting for a psalm

into your watery palms
I pour

drink me in
Kindly

March 2005

91. you and me

To those immured in their temples
Jesus came with message:
 "God is Spirit essence.
Those who worship God
must spirit sacred Presence."

Christians rushed America
with promulgation:
"burn your pagan gods
drink our holy book
while we parcel land God promised us."

Natives sang the higher:
"we feel everywhere great Spirit
whom you name Jesus.
No one who knows this
would dare to conquer sacredness."

What is this between you and me?

92. here you are again

here you are again
sitting on my bed
waiting for my wake

you're always here

for well over forty years
I've had to face you

I've exhausted myself
trying to beat you

I write but my words don't erase you
I run but my feet can't beat you

what is it that you want: defeat? surrender?

must you sit here on my nightbed
waiting for me to recline again
when you've been in my head all day?

isn't it enough?
tally the matches.

Or, are you afraid I'll grab
the spirit of him who didn't give in
and rise up to win the morning?
And maybe I'll do it again tomorrow.

spring 2005

93. clepsydra

No, none of us
have ichor
flowing
in our veins
it's just blood
mixed with water—
and we are water
more than blood.
We deliquesce
in measures
some dripping
quicker than others
some seeming
not to evanesce
but we all do—
in time.
While we argue
of fairness
and unfairness
substance
trickles out—
something heavier
than us stealing
our best.
Strange that
we can't hold back
stranger that we
almost want
the drops to end
and the trial
stop without
any solution.

spring 2005

94. I am earth

I am earth, not angel
the long cavernous sinew, splotched, gnarled.
I am earth, not fire,
a wandering river, restless forest, marled.
I am earth, not air
weightier than water, crumpled, restless, scarred.
I am earth, not spirit
rooted, sandblown, bent, buckled, hard.
I am earth, so much earth
I cling sky, clutch greens, waters hold.
I am earth, dead earth,
alive again, seasoned, seeded, young and old.
I am earth, not heaven hung,
raw and dust, mortal tired, bent and curled.
I am earth, slow and slumped,
blind and spent, giving and gone from.
I am earth, animaled earth
with birds, dogs, whistles and whines.
I am earth, not angel:
spirits come and moan through me as wind.
I am earth, the grave of all,
the hider of secrets, where sorrow stops.
I am earth, fecund and spermed,
seeded, sweetened, soaked, and sunned.
I am earth, blood of rivers
fountainhead of rhythm, ebb and tide.
I am earth, good God alive
with seabreeze, salt, sweat, mud and spit.
I am earth seen, sogged, and sung,
spun through a multitude of rhymes.
I am earth, humaned to death,
about to get palingenesis in second breath.

autumn 2004

95. fling

just as Christ walked in Galilee
so has he moved among the trees
surrounding my air and face
       this is my epiphany. what's yours?

just as Jesus walked the Galilee
so has he skimmed upon the seas
surrounding my beach and face
       this is my epiphany. what's yours?

slim thoughts climb trees to see him pass
old suspicions fish oceans to watch him rise

the last one to see him wrote a book
what's your story? I'll give you mine

just as Jesus flung love like seeds
spread kingdoms with flocks of words
broke religions with hammer and head
       so I fling, spread, break.

seeds multiply. birds migrate. I take
what is left of journeying and move.
I seek what is left of sorrowing and sing
       as I fling, spread, break.

summer 2005

96. passage

what is it between the page and text
beyond the sheet and unimaginable next
that we so chase with amassed words?

everyone must be read after it's been told
the scrawls they left, the scroll they split,
the last glance between couples as they part.

had it been longer, we make ourselves believe,
it would have been epic--should have been
culminated genius exhaustively expressed

and then they left.

we sensed it was a sonnet nearing denoument
about to get to the last line that explains
how we write our way into eternity

but the stanza never ends, just alot of
"if you can imagine" and "I see something"
scribbling its way into blank horizons--

it depends on where you look at the silhouette
whether the stroke slides off the canvas edge
or gets lost in a sein of seagulls winging waves

so hard to stop.

then there's the measure that's never right,
a scrap of that illusive masterpiece begun
and lost and begun again, stretching for

the bridge that ties the lonely bars together--
that ending of a brilliantly light conclusion
where heaven unearths us and gives us tongues

to lilt instead of stuttering what was meant.
for the voyage will have given sight
and perfect sense to all we couldn't rhyme

when we pass time.

and you, our friend, pushed over boundaries,
pioneered lines for others to coast,
left passages not impossible to follow—

and even though perfect is broken at best
with gaps, lacunae, and indecipherableness
of wandering musings you wanted to flesh,

you found ways into his mysteriousness,
passing words your fathers had stopped,
translated past scriptures into sacred places

you never thought.

June 2005
for Kenneth Taylor (1917-2005), creator of the Living Bible,
fellow member of the team that made the *New Living Translation*

97. he moves

He moves between the breaking seas
      in dark mystery.

Pelicans wing along the peeling waves.

The eyes of God, the face of man—
      you are not quite one of us.

The disk drops darkness and it is cold.

He makes eternity palpable, almost
      attainable. Almost.

The clouds eat sunsets and are gone.

He lingers somewhere near the broken
      soul and quiet breath.

Seagulls and pelicans warm winter waters.

Some say he appears as dolphin. As savior
      of the drowning.

Dogs chase waves. Men chase dogs and days.

Too fast. Too swift the kick from here to there.
      But he makes it.

I am not warm enough for winter.

autumn 2005

98. zoa

they've been the mind of the moving Maker living
    in being, spirits of the Spirit, zoapoetic
in shape, flash, metaform, flowing, and glow

    emanations of effulgent procreations,
God's glance and gaze, divine sweep, flutter, soar, and sail
    they rapture us into more and making

they are the thoughts between now gone and next
    the imaginations of children before they're etched
flowing into clouds like angels, ephemeral, wet

they swarm the skies like so many clouds in swirl
    they swash our sight like flamingos lifting in flight
clearer than gods and more serene, they move as lights

    as they aspire from here to there migrating desires
they circle by wing of soul, by thrust of gentleness
    in sun stroke, moon pull, togetherness and glide

they slide between fascinations and sunbeams
    slipping through cracks of clouds, broken leaves,
tottering shelves of sky, heavied by much too much

    they take our thoughts and brave them into otherness
by vault, spring of being, swift skip into muse and make—
    the pounce after pondering, the catch of contemplation—

they are the fetch of imagination, the wing of flight,
    the sight of seeing, the long strong pulse of sacredness,
the apotheosis of promised hopes and inspirations

their wings sing them from wind to flung far—
     the stretch of, the slim leap, the long faith
and reach into elation without pause or ponder

they are afloat, numinous lumens, multiple faces,
     places we've never been, songs we've not yet turned
they seep, smile, send us into longing for words

they thin the membrane between now and ever
     as we unflesh into float, fling, free, rise and slide
almighty, sieving soul through solid heaven

autumn 2005

99. Dia de los Muertos
November 2nd, Angangueo, Mexico
(the day the souls of the dead are carried back to their ancestors)

as I suspend on this mountain in Angangueo
     with myriads salmoning the forest
I reckon I was among the second generation or third
     the late ones birthed under brutal sun.
while the first generation lived gloriously ephemeral
     my generation turned our wings southwest
each journeying alone to the home we'd never been

I migrated a hundred miles each sun and moon
     voyaging seas, crossing sunkilled deserts
gliding breezes, piloted by supernaturalness
     living on God as thin as spirit
flinging wings into open spaces, never stopping
     until I perigrinated to a paradise I can't speak

dangling like angelharp upon this boxtree with millions
        I was sure I had landed perfect Eden
where I could hang limp battered wings
        and give up everything called struggle.
even when winter thinned and many among us fell
        I hung to my immortality. I clung until
spring equinox pushed me into restlessness

I tried with all my will to resist the urge
        to abandon heaven in favor of birth
but the sunlight piercing my thin wings
        as stainedglass windows in a cathedral
wooed me to move to the summer milkweed
        where I layed down my seed and hope
and winged off to the carolina coast

as the sun got fiercer, my wings withered
        and I fell down flat as earth flat as beach
flat as sea flat as two sheets pressed together
        like ancient papyri in an Egyptian coffin

a child running the sea picked me up
        in his trembling fingers and threw me into wind
I rose and dropped and landed in the surf
        sucking me out a lifeless leaf
until the turning tide pushed me ashore
        limp, watersoaked, rolled up like a bulla

an old man walking the sea picked me up
        in his trembling fingers and blew me into wind
and that is why I am here again
        suspended on this mountain in Angangueo

November 2, 2005

100. january

in january, another late january, you have to give way
to sadness. you have to admit mortality and endings.
that's what january does. you can hold on in December,
get drunk and numb. you can believe all kinds of things
if you want to, if you try. but january transmogrifies.
there are no myths in january. you are cold and old and
getting older. and january says so. oh, you can hope spring.
we all do. but january says mourn. blessed are those
who take a sip of the grey day, the sunless day,
drink brittleness into their bones and mourn. make promises
that you will always slurp summer and always smile.
but for now, mourn, because it is january the dead grass says.
the cold ocean moans. the seagulls look for slim fish
and look hungry because it is january and there are none.

January 2006

101. un-omniscience

Outside our windows stormclouds razored the sky,
slicing it to shreds of darkness. Lightning lashed the night
like some punitive master making all creatures rush for cover.
As the stormwinds stomped furiously and rains clobbered
everything green, I moaned, "there's gotta be a better way to nourish earth
than terror falling on our heads." While theodicies rumbled in my mind,
a call away our son was pinned under an overturned jeep—
just down the street—but we didn't hear his cries for help
(this un-omniscience has robbed my sleep). We didn't see him facing the edge
nor ease his pain as he gasped for breath. We couldn't be his savior
whom he was readying himself to see. Nor did we know how
he was anguishing our anguish when we would be told his fate.
I can't believe we slept that night and didn't know till light
made morning that an unknown neighbor heard him calling.

July 15, 2006 (for Peter after his accident, from his parents)

134

102. twisted

the torso's bent
in crazy crooks
of twists
and turns
in search of sun
by bend of wind

so has the journey been

not the towering pines
which straightway
penetrate fecund sky

I have warped my way
among the masses
in thirst of any kind light

my roots sinking to tangled darkness

I have breathed winter
and heaved winter time and again
(count them iced on my rings)
I have weaved among elms more gnarled than

and sucked the teets of sun

I have been slanted
by tilted wind
in sideway seas
wind as strong as sun
wind as thin as him
who walks wind

he passes

my roots still tangle with darkness
wet with worming through hades

I snarl

he passes again
on his way back
from walking woods
in other places

I sere

he sees me again
in another broken season
that I am still snarled
bending and twisting
spitting through the clumps
for a drink of light

he sits
beneath my boughs
and whistles
he sleeps
and does not ask
my name

he counts
my spindly shadows
he counts them long
he thins
and disappears

I twist yet again
silently
as though nothing
moved
but it did
like night
turning day

he comes again

from walking seas
from walking woods
he passes

like wind
like waves
like sundusk

he sees I have twisted again
he sees I have broken into light
with bud, bloom, and bend

my roots tangle with soiled darkness

my torso twists
my leaves mingle with light
angels of light
winging through woods

my branches
are heavy with light
heavy with darkness
heavy with hanging

I keep earth in place

my bare branches
know he's passing
my barkless trunk
knows he's sitting
counting my rings

he sings
he leaves
he calls
my name
after him

I twist I turn

but he's gone
way too long
a winter
never passing

I imagine
he's sitting
among others
who still
arch and bend

I imagine
he's sitting
on branches
of others
stooping with fruit

my roots have dried up darkness

I break before
I penetrate
any heaven

I fall in pieces
degenerate
limb by limb
as slowly
and awkwardly
as I began

I am thinner than shadows

I am thinner than light

I am heavier than darkness

I am pecked
and hollowed
stripped of every kindness

yet I still stand
and feel him coming
as he walks
the wind

he sits beside me
coos my name
cradles me
back and forth
back and forth
until I am earthed again

February 2006

103. monarchs

it's early October in Carolina
when creatures metaphysic south
most in broods and pools:
pelicans, cormorants, egrets
arrowing blue heavens

spots, whitings, blues
chased by black cold and sharks.
my instincts tell me follow
but there's no way to morph
unless I quickly wing or fin

somehow crysalis uncocoons
from pupa darkness with wings
colored sunrise and surprise:
there is transfiguration—
God can change after all

leaving behind shed
blood and skin these miracles
fling into translucent cherubim—
metamorphosis in flight
gives us rise to sing!

as I worm along the beach
one by one they flit pass
magnificent every few minutes
following the coast religiously
on some appointed route

I gaze at their salmon wings
painted with black auspice
praying to divine the sign
as each alone pilgrims
to a home it's never been

October is nearly over
I hear the weather falling
fear the failing sun
they're gone like souls
disappeared and sainted

but I remember a few weeks
ago watching their noiseless wings
move them quicker than waves
and I'm braved to imagine a place
even God would like to live

if they know where to fly
at summer's end shouldn't I
sense when paradise begins
and lift imago wings
to austral winds and rise?

yes! when the call comes
to uncocoon and unfurl
diaphanous wings thin as angels
flying nowhere near imagination
I will split, flare, and wend

October 2006

104. graced

I studied your words and I studied your face—
both spoke of love for God and life of grace.
I saw in you an attractive blend of textual scholar
and servant of the Word. It was eminently clear
you had applied yourself wholly to the Scriptures
and applied the Scriptures wholly to yourself.

I, like you, studied the ancient manuscripts
to recover the original New Testament text.
I also shared your passion to translate the Bible
for English readers. I am inspired by your example
to know the Lord Jesus who spirited his word
and I aspire to express him in action and truth.

As you graced those of us who knew your essence,
may the Lord grace you with his eternal presence.

February 18, 2007
For Bruce Metzger (1914-2007)
who greatly encouraged me
to pursue my studies of the New Testament text
and who inspired me to live a life pleasing to God

105. thirst

the sun throats in its burning
in a billion years it will gulp desert-earth

thirst is a strange creature
it is the wanting to be living

I thirst
sometimes I don't know what for—
to swallow new earth, drink a planet
pure as liquid God

then thirst is good
it is the wanting to be living

the moon moans in its mooring
soon it will be unanchored and freed
to float wherever

there goes our sea swallowing earth
but never can it swallow thirst

I will not compare you to sun
I will not say you're moon
or imagine you're ocean

stronger than ocean
longer than sun
fuller than moon

life is the mightiest thirst

summer 2007

106. this is my ink

The paper I inscribe, a transfigured pine,
is flatter now but no less tree to speak. Resin runs down my quill. Wings fly
across my page flashing shadows of some distant sun.
Or is it cuttlefish squirting jetblack fluid?
I am swimming for words when caught in a squalled sunrise.
A torrent flush treads the beach, bends fronds,
marches from the nor'east angry at nothing I know.
I can't see the light stars birthed four billion years ago. There's half
a million left to break. But I see the wind when it begins to sing.
And this is my ink.

I grab some sun and smear it across the face.
Tall light is better. Mixed color. Limbs limn a dream I've seen. Long after
I've hugged the night, I wake to watergreen trees stretching.
Or are they behemoths etched on caves?
I am tunneling for signs when trapped in an ancient earthquake.
A tsunami erupts over the cliffs, breaks Atlantis,
plunges a civilization into obfuscation.
I can't see the waves some faults spit thousands of years ago. There's half
a million left to break. But I see the wind when it begins to sing.
And this is my ink.

Dark clouds glorify the sun. They are fluid pilgrims
launching flights I've never winged. Singing is the fix to sorrow. Tomorrow
I'll get blown over in the storm surge, tumbled in bad waves.
Or is it that I will turn rain again?
I'm worming through libraries lost to ghosts and storms
trying to resurrect dead tomes from flattened pages
when another hurricane comes named Anastasia.
I can't see the whirl Africa pumped thousands of hours ago. There's half
a million left to break. But I see the wind when it begins to sing.
And this is my ink.

summer 2007

144